ABC's of the Bible

God's Word Through the Alphabet

Glen R. Landin

Copyright © 2017 Glen R. Landin

No part of this publication may be reproduced or transmitted in any form or by any means, electronic or mechanical, including photocopying, recording, or by any information storage or retrival system without written permission from the author.

Scriptures NIV
All scripture is God-breathed and is useful for teaching, rebuking, correcting, and training in righteousness, so that the man of God may be thoroughly equipped for every good work. 2 Timothy 3:17

Creative Artistic Publishing
www.CreativeArtisticPublishing.com
Orange, California

ISBN – 13 978 0996280754
ISBN – 10 0996280758

Printed Edition June 2017

Printed in the United States of America

glen_landin@mail.com
www.GlenLandin.com

The "ABC's of the Bible" makes learning and understanding The Holy Bible easier for children. This book includes Bible words, corresponding short verses, silhouette Bibles, and fill in the words on each page. The selected verses chosen were taken from the NIV Bible. Perfect for children of all ages to learn and grow in God's Word through the alphabet.

GLEN R. LANDIN

ABC'S OF THE BIBLE

Abba

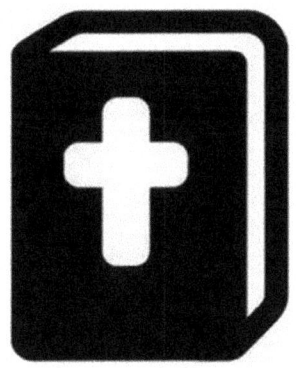

Because you are his sons, God sent the Spirit who calls out; "Abba, Father." Galatians 4:6

GLEN R. LANDIN

Abide

Whenever you enter a house, stay there until you leave that town. Mark 6:10

ABC'S OF THE BIBLE

Alter

I will not violate my covenant or alter what my lips have uttered. Psalms 89:34

GLEN R. LANDIN

Amen

To whom be glory for ever and ever. Amen. Galatians 1:5

Angel

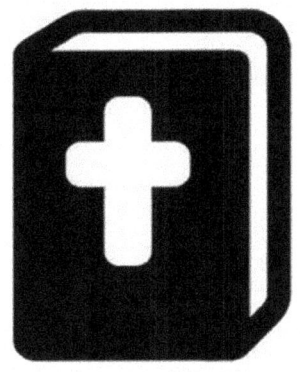

But the angel said to them, "Do not be afraid. I bring you good news of great joy that will be for all the people. Luke 2:10

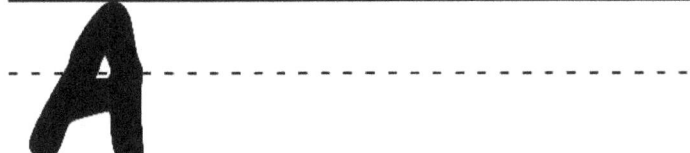

GLEN R. LANDIN

Apostles

The apostles gathered around Jesus and reported to him all they had done and taught.
Mark 6:30

Ark

Male and female, came to Noah and entered the ark, as God had commanded Noah. Genesis 7:9

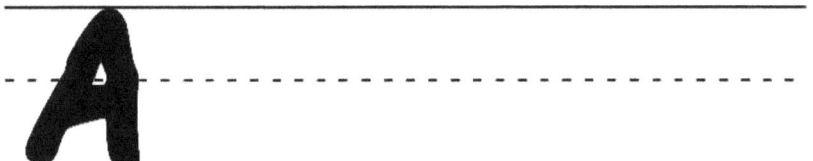

GLEN R. LANDIN

Baptize

Although in fact it was not Jesus who baptized, but his disciples.
John 4:2

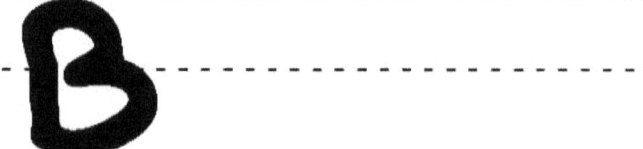

ABC'S OF THE BIBLE

Bethlehem

He sent them to Bethlehem and said, "Go and make a careful search for the child...
Matthew 2:8

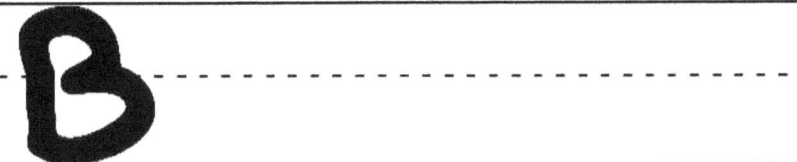

GLEN R. LANDIN

Birth

"She will give birth to a son, and you are to give him the name Jesus, because he will save his people... Matthew 1:21

ABC'S OF THE BIBLE

Bless

"The LORD bless you and keep you," Numbers 6:24

GLEN R. LANDIN

Christ

Jesus Christ is the same yesterday and today and forever. Hebrews 13:8

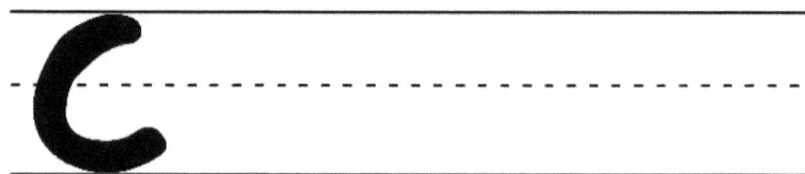

ABC'S OF THE BIBLE

Commands

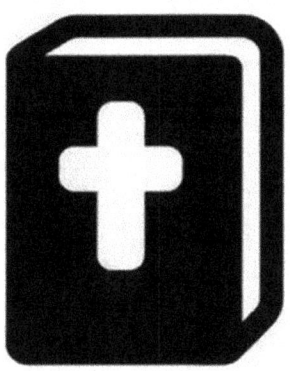

"If you love me, keep my commands." John 14:15

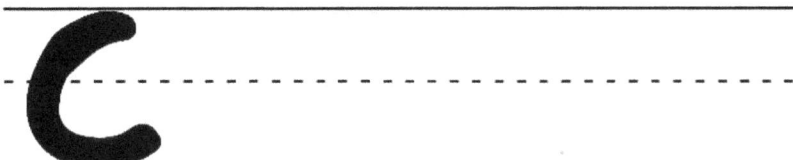

GLEN R. LANDIN

Confess

If we confess our sins, he is faithful and just and will forgive us our sins and purify us... 1 John 1:9

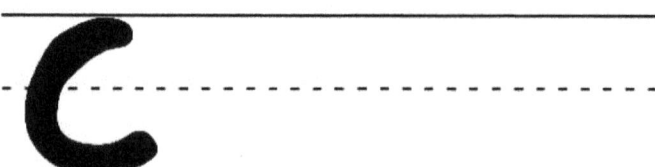

Creation

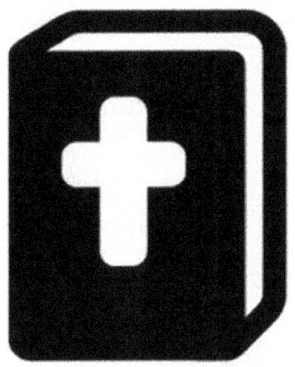

Therefore, if anyone is in Christ, the new creation has come: The old has gone, the new is here!
2 Corinthians 5:17

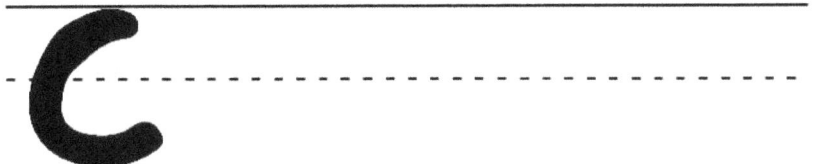

GLEN R. LANDIN

Cross

And whoever does not carry their cross and follow me cannot be my disciple. Luke **14:27**

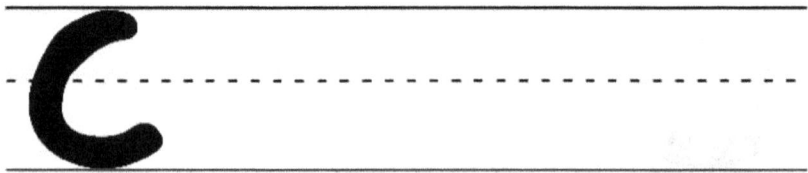

ABC'S OF THE BIBLE

Crown

They put a purple robe on him, then twisted together a crown of thorns and set it on him.
Mark 15:17

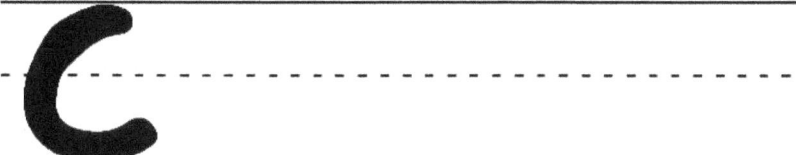

GLEN R. LANDIN

Crucify

...they took off the robe and put his own clothes on him. Then they led him away to crucify him. Matthew 27:31

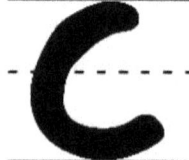

ABC'S OF THE BIBLE

Deliver

And lead us not into temptation, but deliver us from the evil one.
Matthew 6:13

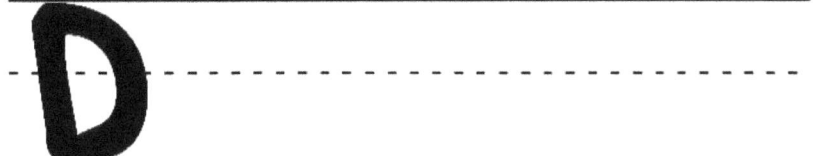

GLEN R. LANDIN

Devotion

But you even undermine piety and hinder devotion to God.
Job 15:4

Disciple

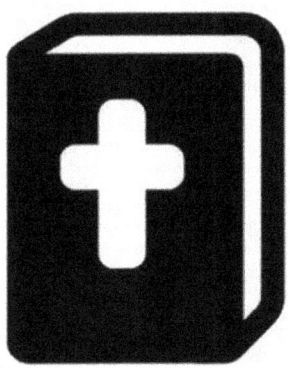

So Peter and the other disciple started for the tomb. John 20:3

GLEN R. LANDIN

Eden

The LORD God took the man and put him in the Garden of Eden to work it and take care of it. Genesis 2:15

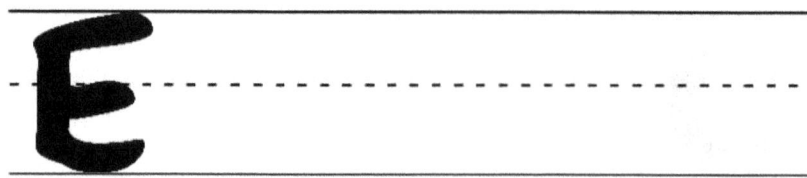

ABC'S OF THE BIBLE

Elder

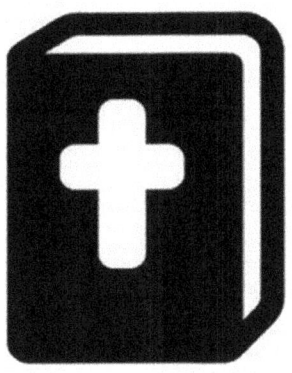

To the elders among you, I appeal as a fellow elder and a witness of Christ's sufferings...
1 Peter 5:1

GLEN R. LANDIN

Eternal

For the wages of sin is death, but the gift of God is eternal life in Christ Jesus our Lord.
Romans 6:23

Faith

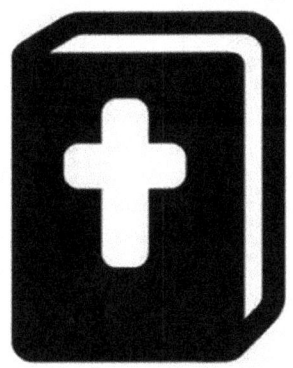

For it is by grace you have been saved, through faith and this is not from yourselves, it is the gift of God. Ephesians 2:8

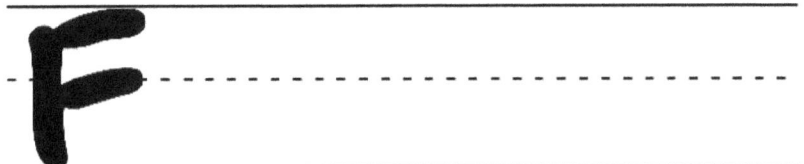

GLEN R. LANDIN

Favor

And as Jesus grew up, he increased in wisdom and in favor with God and people. Luke 2:52

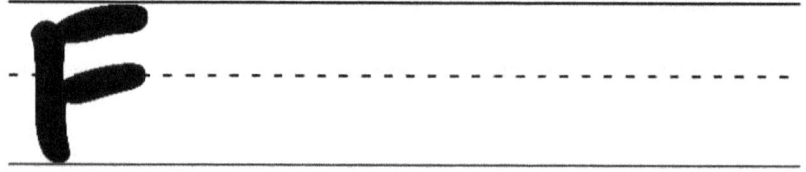

Flesh

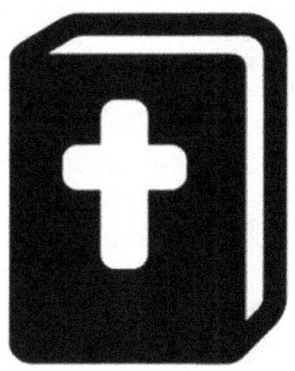

"...This bread is my flesh, which I will give for the life of the world." John 6:51

GLEN R. LANDIN

Forgive

But if you do not forgive, neither will your Father in heaven forgive your failings and shortcomings. Mark 11:26

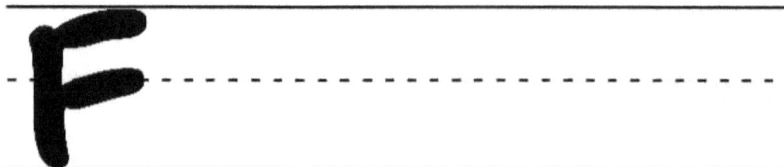

ABC'S OF THE BIBLE

Frankincense

..."Take fragrant spices — gum resin, onycha and galbanum — and pure frankincense, all in equal amounts." Exodus 30:34

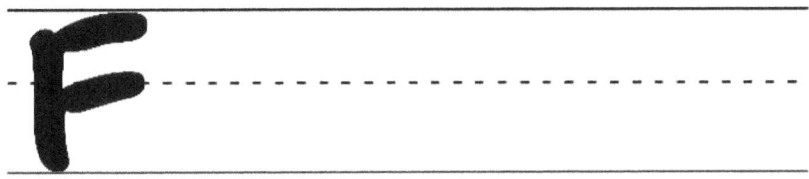

GLEN R. LANDIN

Gentile

There is neither Jew nor Gentile, neither slave nor free, neither male nor female...
Galatians 3:28

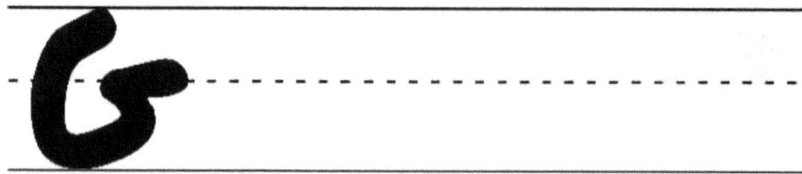

ABC'S OF THE BIBLE

Glory

For all have sinned and fall short of the glory of God.
Romans 3:23

GLEN R. LANDIN

In the beginning was the Word, and the Word was with God, and the Word was God. John 1:1

ABC'S OF THE BIBLE

Gospel

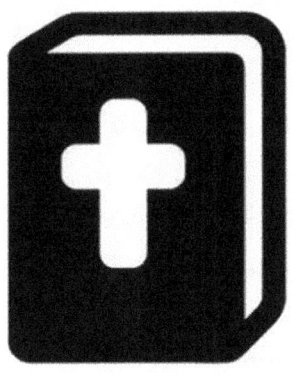

He said to them, "Go into all the world and preach the gospel to all creation." Mark 16:15

GLEN R. LANDIN

Grace

Grace and peace to you from God our Father and the Lord Jesus Christ. 2 Corinthians 1:2

ABC'S OF THE BIBLE

Heaven

In the beginning God created the heavens and the earth.
Genesis 1:1

GLEN R. LANDIN

Holy

Make every effort to live in peace with everyone and to be holy... Hebrews 12:14

Hope

While we wait for the blessed hope — the appearing of the glory of our great God and Savior, Jesus Christ. Titus 2:13

GLEN R. LANDIN

Hosanna

Those who went ahead and those who followed shouted, "Hosanna!" "Blessed is he who comes in the name of the Lord!" Mark 11:9

ABC'S OF THE BIBLE

Hymns

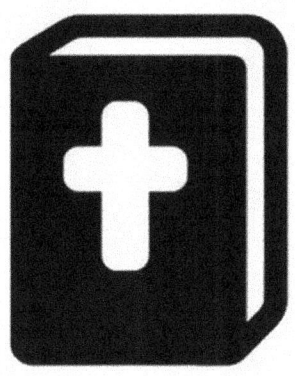

Speaking to one another with psalms, hymns, and songs from the Spirit... Ephesians 5:19

GLEN R. LANDIN

Immanuel

...The virgin will conceive and give birth to a son, and will call him Immanuel. Isaiah 7:14

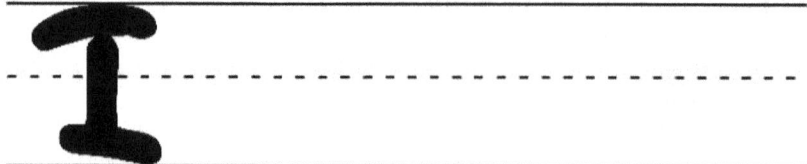

Incense

And when the time for the burning of incense came, all the assembled worshipers were praying outside. Luke **1:10**

GLEN R. LANDIN

Israel

Hear, O Israel; The LORD our God, the LORD is one.
Deuteronomy 6:4

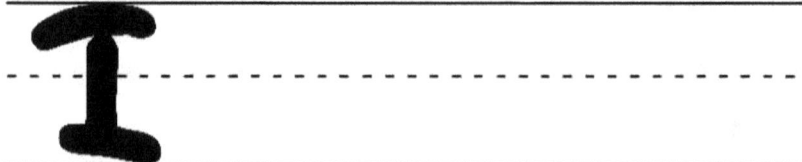

Jerusalem

After Jesus was born in Bethlehem in Judea, during the time of King Herod, Magi from the east came to Jerusalem.
Matthew 2:1

GLEN R. LANDIN

Jesus

Jesus answered, "I am the way and the truth and the life. No one comes to the Father except through me." John 14:6

Joy

Consider it pure joy, my brothers and sisters, whenever you face trials of many kinds. James 1:2

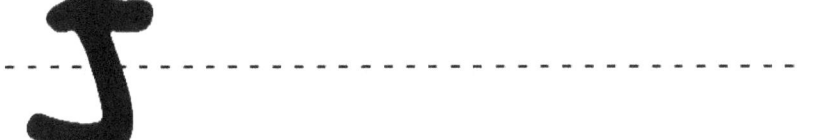

GLEN R. LANDIN

Judge

For the LORD is our judge, the LORD is our lawgiver, the LORD is our king; it is he who will save us. Isaiah 33:22

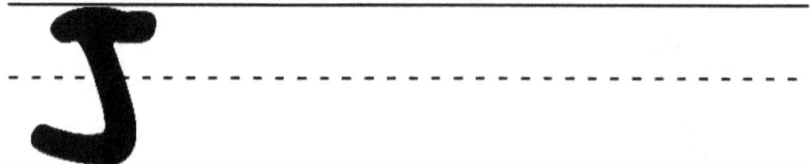

ABC'S OF THE BIBLE

King

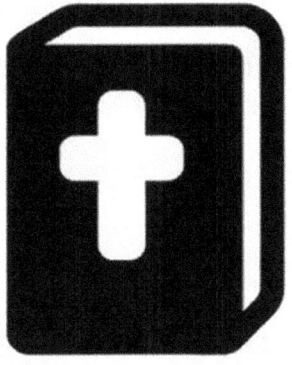

"Blessed is the King who comes in the name of the Lord!" "Peace in heaven and glory in the highest!"
Luke 19:38

GLEN R. LANDIN

Kingdom

Jesus replied, "Very truly I tell you, no one can see the Kingdom of God without being born again."
John 3:3

ABC'S OF THE BIBLE

Lamb

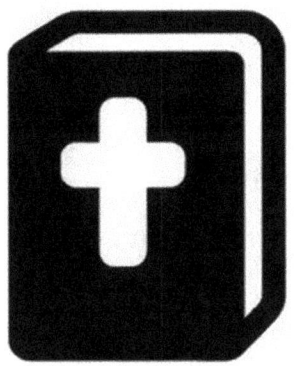

Then came the day of Unleavened Bread on which the Passover lamb had to be sacrificed. Luke 22:7

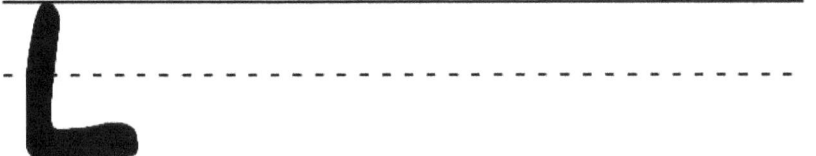

GLEN R. LANDIN

Leper

A man with with leprosy came and knelt before him and said, "Lord, if you are willing, you can make me clean." Matthew 8:2

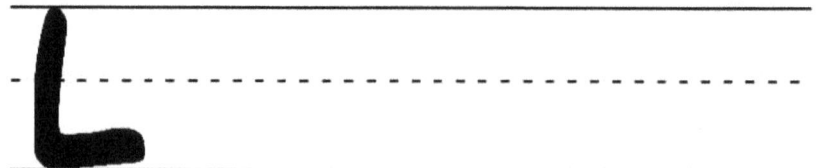

Lord

If you declare with your mouth, "Jesus is Lord," and believe in your heart that God raised him...
Romans 10:9

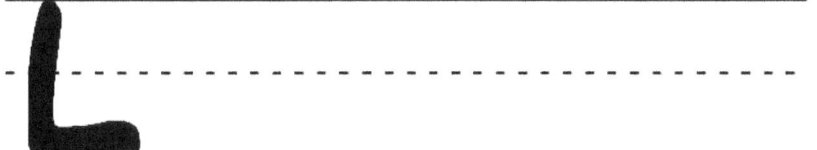

GLEN R. LANDIN

Love

"A new command I give you: Love one another. As I have loved you, so you must love one another." John 13:34

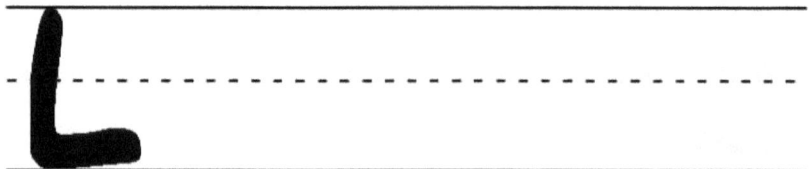

ABC'S OF THE BIBLE

Magi

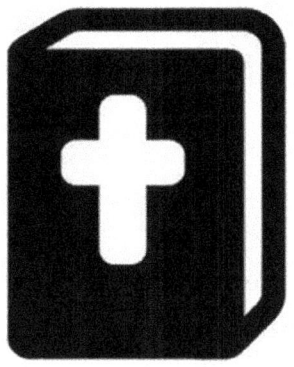

Then Herod called the Magi secretly and found out from them the exact time the star had appeared. Matthew 2:7

GLEN R. LANDIN

Manger

"This will be a sign to you: You will find a baby wrapped in cloths and lying in a manger." Luke 2:12

Manna

The people of Israel called the bread manna. It was white like coriander seed and tasted like wafers made with honey.
Exodus 16:31

GLEN R. LANDIN

Meek

Blessed are the meek, for they will inherit the earth.
Matthew 5:5

ABC'S OF THE BIBLE

Mercy

Therefore, since through God's mercy we have this ministry, we do not lose heart.
2 Corinthians 4:1

GLEN R. LANDIN

Messiah

Everyone who believes that Jesus is the Messiah is born of God, and everyone who loves the Father loves his child as well.
1 John 5:1

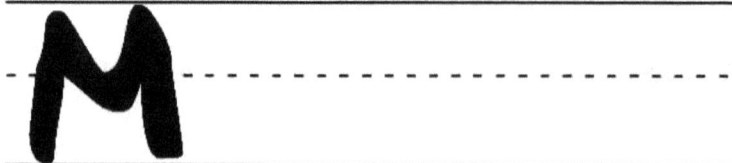

ABC'S OF THE BIBLE

Miracle

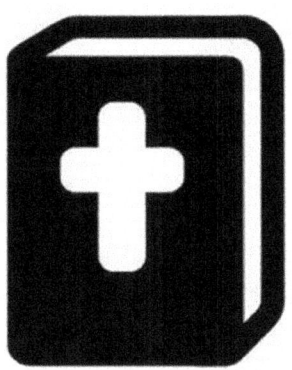

Jesus said to them, "I did one miracle, and you are all amazed."
John 7:21

GLEN R. LANDIN

Myrrh

...Then they opened their treasures and presented him with gifts of gold, frankincense, and myrrh. Matthew 2:11

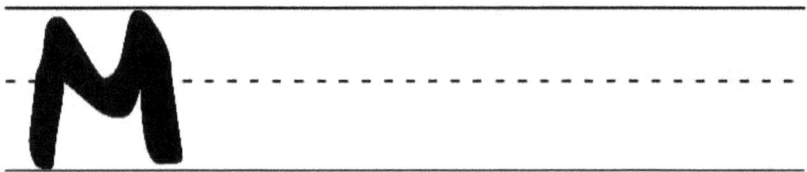

ABC'S OF THE BIBLE

Nativity

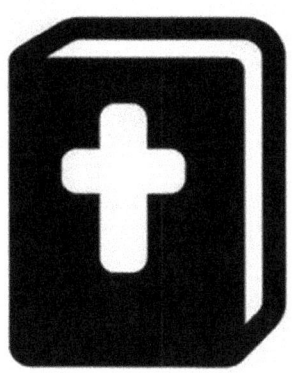

"This is what the Sovereign LORD says to Jerusalem: Your ancestry and birh were in the land of the Canaanites... Ezekiel 16:3

GLEN R. LANDIN

Nazareth

"Jesus of Nazareth," they replied. "I am he," Jesus said.
John 18

ABC'S OF THE BIBLE

Obey

Children, obey your parents in the Lord, for this is right.
Ephesians 6:1

GLEN R. LANDIN

Offering

"These are the regulations for the fellowship offering anyone may present to the LORD."
Leviticus 7:11

ABC'S OF THE BIBLE

Olives

Jesus went out as usual to the Mount of Olives, and his disciples followed him. Luke 22:39

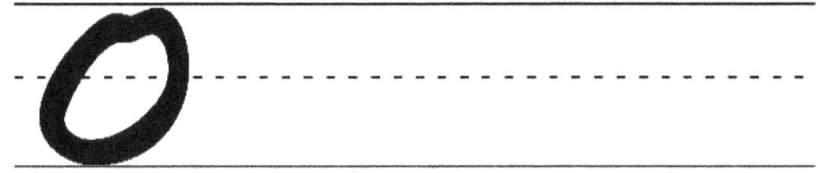

GLEN R. LANDIN

Parables

When Jesus had finished these parables, he moved on from there. Matthew 13:53

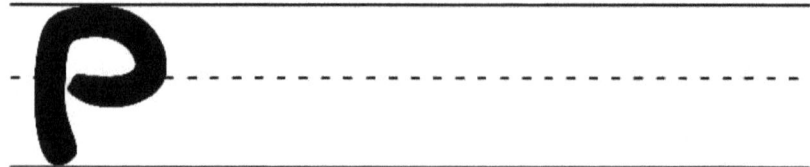

ABC'S OF THE BIBLE

Passover

...went into the city and found things just as Jesus had told them. So they prepared the Passover. Mark 14:16

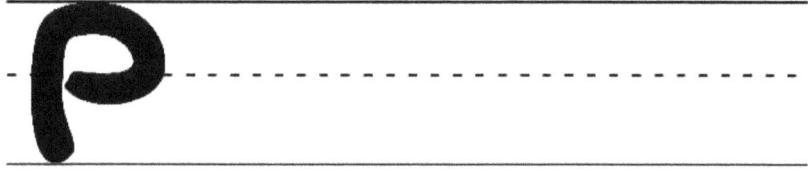

GLEN R. LANDIN

Peace

Grace and peace to you from God our Father and the Lord Jesus Christ. 2 Corinthians 1:2

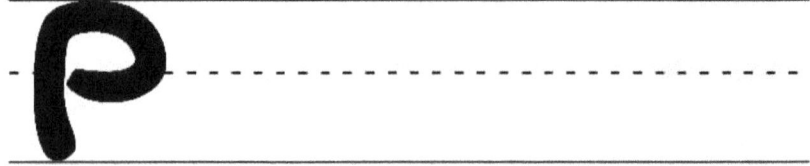

ABC'S OF THE BIBLE

Praise

I praise you because I am fearfully and wonderfully made; your works are wonderful...
Psalms 139:14

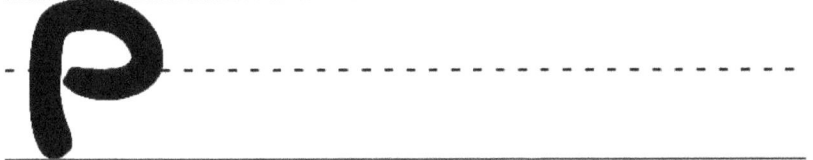

GLEN R. LANDIN

Prayer

Therefore I tell you, whatever you ask for in prayer, believe that you have received it...
Mark 11:24

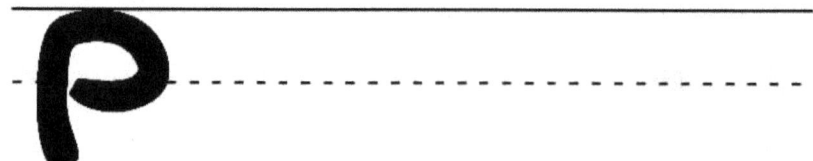

ABC'S OF THE BIBLE

Prophet

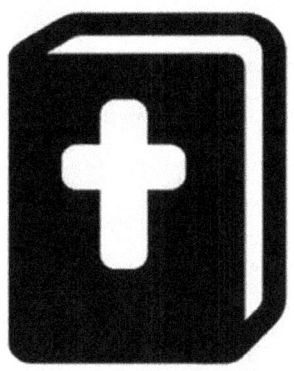

All this took place to fulfill what the Lord had said through the prophet. Matthew 1:22

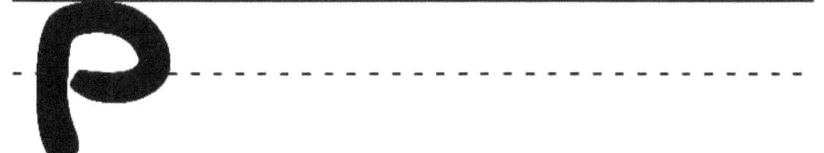

GLEN R. LANDIN

Queen

Say to the king and to the queen mother, "Come down from your thrones, for your glorious crowns will fall from your heads."
Jeremiah 13:18

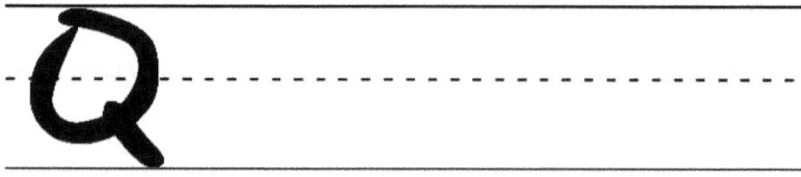

Redeem

Into your hands I commit my spirit; redeem me, LORD, my faithful God. Psalms 31:15

GLEN R. LANDIN

Renew

Restore us to yourself, LORD, that we may return; renew our days as of old.
Lamentations 5:21

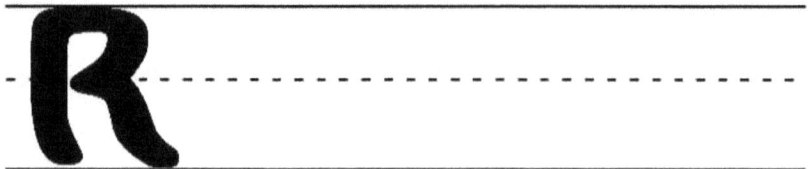

ABC'S OF THE BIBLE

Repent

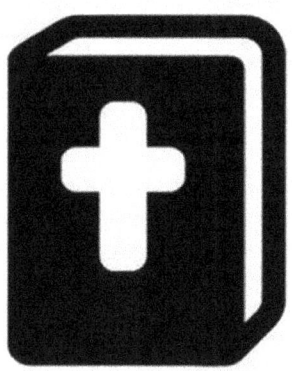

They went out and preached that people should repent.
Mark 6:12

GLEN R. LANDIN

Risen

He is not here; he has risen, just as he said. Come and see the place where he lay.
Matthew 28:6

ABC'S OF THE BIBLE

Roman

In those days Caesar Augustus issued a decree that a census should be taken of the entire Roman world. Luke 2:1

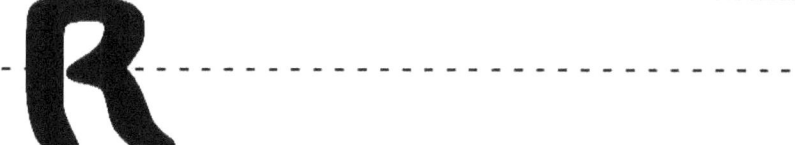

GLEN R. LANDIN

Sabbath

"Remember the Sabbath day by keeping it holy." Exodus 20:8

Sacrifice

And by that will, we have been made holy through the sacrifice of the body of Jesus Christ once for all. Hebrews 10:10

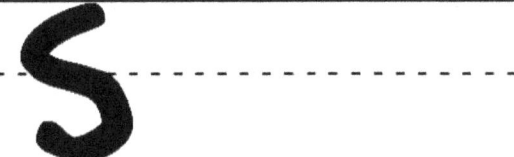

GLEN R. LANDIN

Salvation

For the grace of God has appeared that offers salvation to all people. Titus 2:11

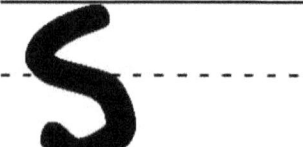

ABC'S OF THE BIBLE

Savior

And we have seen and testify that the Father has sent his Son to be the savior of the world. **1 John 4:14**

GLEN R. LANDIN

Scrolls

When you come, bring the cloak that I left with Carpus at Troas, and my scrolls, especially the parchments. 2 Timothy 4:13

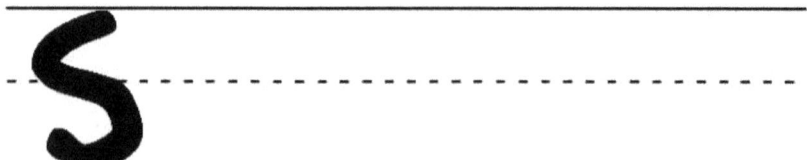

ABC'S OF THE BIBLE

Seals

...who sat on the throne a scroll with writing on both sides and sealed with seven seals.
Revelation 5:1

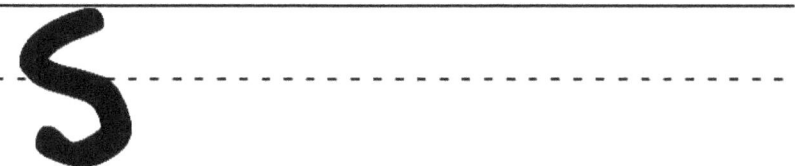

GLEN R. LANDIN

Sins

Therefore confess your sins to each other and pray for each other so that you may be healed. James 5:16

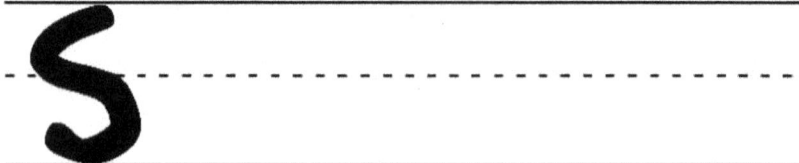

Spirit

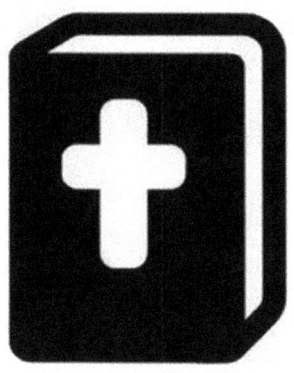

But the fruit of the Spirit is love, joy, peace, patience, kindess, goodness, faithfulness.
Galatians 5:22

Staff

...I will fear no evil, for you are with me; your rod and your staff, they comfort me.
Psalms 23:4

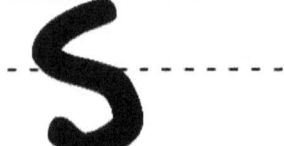

ABC'S OF THE BIBLE

Tablets

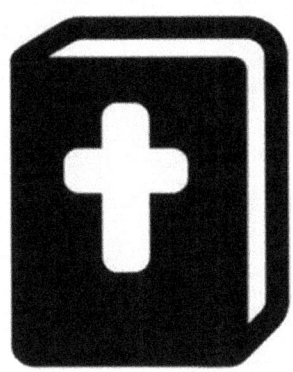

The tablets were the work of God; the writing was the writing of God, engraved on the tablets. Exodus 32:16

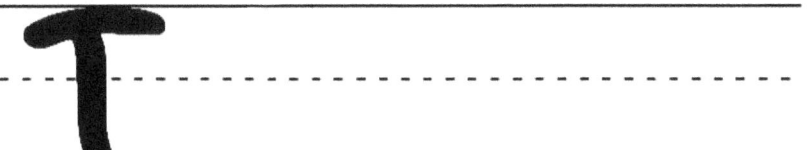

GLEN R. LANDIN

Temple

Jesus answered them, "Destroy this temple, and I will raise it again in three days." John 2:19

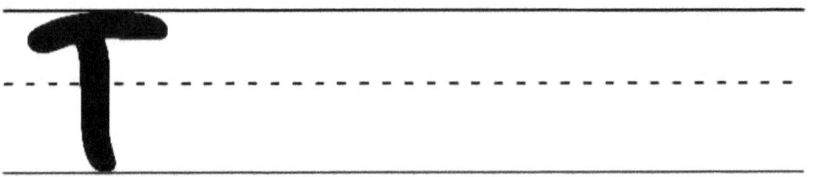

Tomb

Finally the other disciple, who had reached the tomb first, also went inside. He saw and believed.
John 20:8

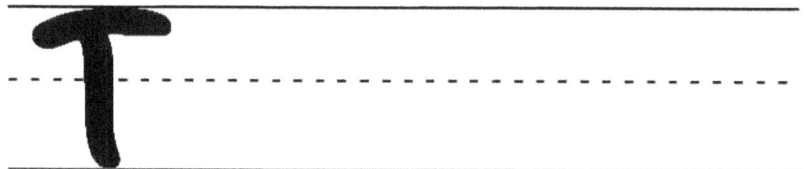

GLEN R. LANDIN

Truth

Jesus answered, "I am the way and the truth and the life. No one comes to the Father except through me." John 14:6

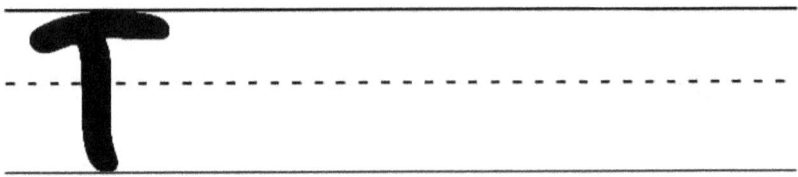

ABC'S OF THE BIBLE

Unity

Make every effort to keep the unity of the Spirit through the bond of peace. Ephesians 4:3

GLEN R. LANDIN

Vashti

But when the attendants delivered the King's command, Queen Vashti refused to come...
Esther 1:2

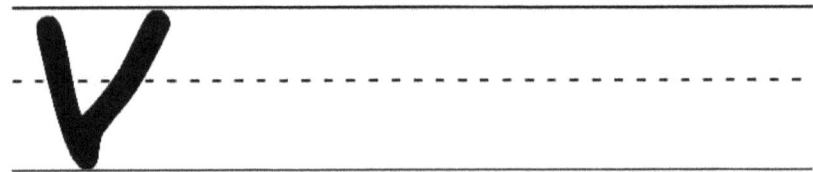

Victory

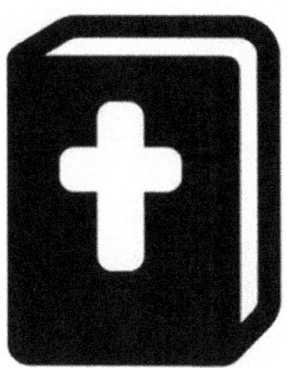

For the LORD takes delight in his people; he crowns the humble with victory. Psalms 149:4

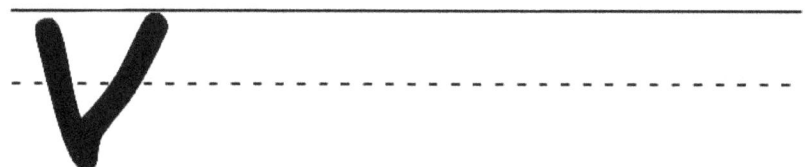

GLEN R. LANDIN

Vineyard

The vineyard of the LORD Almighty is the house of Israel, and the people of Judah are the vines... Isaiah 5:7

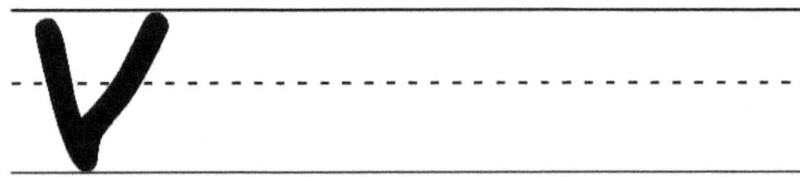

ABC'S OF THE BIBLE

Witness

He came as a witness to testify concerning that light, so that through him all might believe.
John 1:7

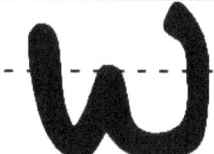

GLEN R. LANDIN

Word

For the Word of God is alive and active. Sharper than any double-edged sword...
Hebrews 4:12

ABC'S OF THE BIBLE

Worship

Come, let us bow down in worship, let us kneel before the LORD our Maker. Psalms 95:6

GLEN R. LANDIN

Xerxes

This is what happened during the time of Xerxes, the Xerxes who ruled over 127 provinces...
Esther 1:1

ABC'S OF THE BIBLE

Yoke

Take my yoke upon you and learn from me, for I am gentle and humble in heart... Matthew 11:29

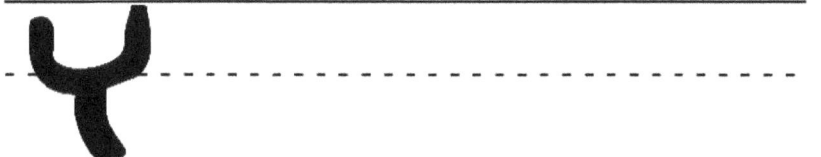

GLEN R. LANDIN

Zeal

Never be lacking in zeal, but keep your spiritual fervor, serving the Lord. Romans 12:11

Z

ABC'S OF THE BIBLE

Zion

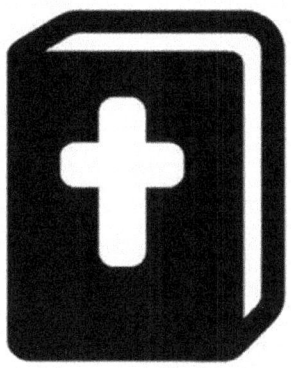

Nevertheless, David captured the fortress of Zion — which is the City of David. 2 Samuel 5:7

Z

GLEN R. LANDIN

About The Author

Glen Landin continues writing unique and informative books. In this children's release entitled, "ABC's of the Bible", he combines simple terms from the Bible which includes short verses, fill in the the words, and a silhouette Bible on each page.

As a creative writer, author, artist, and photographer, he also enjoys interior design, model railroading, visual displays, and traveling.

Through Glen's creative writing skills, poems, phrases, affirmations, Bible verses, and messages; he inspires, encourages, and motivates people to remain positive, thankful, strong, and blessed! Because all things are possible to those who believe! Amen

www.ingramcontent.com/pod-product-compliance
Lightning Source LLC
Chambersburg PA
CBHW071720040426
42446CB00011B/2143